Your Family Journey

Your Family Journey

A guide to building faith at home

Cover design: Tracy Watkins
Cover photos copyright © by iStockphoto. All rights reserved.
ISBN: 978-1-58997-520-0

Note: Portions of this book are adapted from *Parents' Guide to the Spiritual Growth of Children* (Focus on the Family/Tyndale House Publishers, 2000) and *Parents' Guide to the Spiritual Mentoring of Teens* (Focus on the Family/Tyndale House Publishers, 2001). Contributors include Paul Batura, Jeff Hoyle, Cory Albracht, John Duckworth, Larry Weeden, Lissa Halls Johnson, Joe White, Jim Weidmann, Kurt Bruner, John Trent, Rick Osborne, K. Christie Bowler, and Kevin Miller.

Printed in the United States of America
1 2 3 4 5 6 7 / 15 14 13 12 11 10 09

**To obtain a discussion guide for this book, please go to
www.yourfamilyjourney.com.**

Contents

Foreword vii

Part I: The Journey Begins

1. Why Plan Your Journey? 1

2. Where Do You Want to End Up? 7

3. What Are You and Your Family Like? 17

4. Making Your Plan: Mission, Goals, and Action Steps 27

5. A Covenant You Can Keep 37

Part II: Staying on Course

6. Tools You Can Use 43

7. Helping Kids Reach the Next Level 51

8. Helping Teens Get Where They're Going 61

Troubleshooting 71

Creating Your Family Covenant at a Glance 81

Your Worksheet . . . . see end-of-book insert

Foreword

I attended a conference a number of years ago where Peter Benson, Director of Search Institute, made a statement that challenged my perspective and approach to ministry. He said, "As the family goes, so goes the future of the church. Religious life in the home is more influential than the church."

Take a moment to consider this statement. How are families "going" today? If the future of the church really hinges on the current health and stability of families, then what does our future look like? Secondly, if religious life in the home is more influential, then why do we focus so much of our time, energy, and resources on what takes place at church?

I think we all realize that families are struggling today. That's because the enemy has moved his attack into individual households. He knows that by destroying faith life in the home, he can cause hurt, pain, and alienation that will keep people away from God and the church for generations.

Studies already show that prayer, Bible reading, and faith-talk don't take place in most Christian families. Like the rest of our consumer-driven, outsourcing society, we've become dependent on "experts"—in this case, the church—to be the primary place that teaches and develops faith. As a result, many of our young adults are walking away from Christianity. For them, faith was something they did in a church building or program—not a relationship they lived out 24 hours a day at home.

To make matters worse, a lot of us are three to four generations removed from the last that made home and parents the primary nurturers of faith. As a result, many parents no longer know how to make true Christian living part of life at home.

I'm not saying that today's parents are bad. In fact, I believe many of them are desperately seeking to raise their children in better households than the ones in which they grew up. They may even agree that Christianity has the one thing *all* families need to succeed: Jesus Christ in the center of every household. But they're also saying, "I don't know how to do this, because this was not something I experienced."

Perhaps the most important question we can ask is this: How much time, energy, and resources are we investing to make the home the primary place where faith is nurtured? We've invested much in things we do at church; maybe it's time to invest in what's happening in the home.

What I love about *Your Family Journey* is that it's a practical tool that can be used to bring true Christian living back home. If we want things to change, we have to move away from quick-fix programs and one-hour Christianity to true lifestyle transformation. We have to help families create a picture and plan for how they'll live out their faith every day and every week. *Your Family Journey* helps us do just that!

The enemy has a plan for what he wants to accomplish: to take Christ and Christlike living out of the home. Do we have a plan to bring Jesus back into the very center of every household? It's time for the church to reestablish the home as the primary place where faith is to be nurtured. That means making faith at home a top priority.

—Pastor Mark Holmen
Author, *Faith Begins at Home* and *Building Faith at Home*

CHAPTER 1

Why Plan Your Journey?

He knew where he wanted to go—but when he died, he didn't even know where he'd been.

Who was he? An addict? A nomad? A sleepwalker? Not quite.

In the spring of 1486, Italian explorer Christopher Columbus was granted an audience with the reigning monarchs of Spain. His request was straightforward but bold. Convinced he could discover a shorter westward trade route to the Orient, he sought three ships and funding for a year's exploration.

At first the request was denied. The royal court's advisors dismissed Columbus's navigational calculations. They also didn't understand why he wanted to travel *west* in order to land in the *East*. But Columbus was persistent, and apparently persuasive, too. In 1492 his wish was granted.

As many schoolchildren know, Columbus never did find what he was looking for. Instead he stumbled upon the New World, landing in the Bahamas in a place he named San Salvador.

After crossing the Atlantic eight times, he was confined to his bed by a crippling case of arthritis. He died of a heart attack in 1506, still convinced that he'd discovered a chain of islands off the Asian mainland. Reality suggests otherwise, of course; he'd missed his target by thousands of miles.

Some might suggest he was lucky. Everyone would agree he was wrong. But why did he miss his mark so completely?

Columbus had relied on a chart and compass, but all his calculations were based on a drastically low guess at the earth's circumference. Compounding his mistake, he erroneously figured his distance by estimating his speed, then multiplying it by the number of times the sand had passed through an hourglass.

Confused? So was Columbus!

And so it goes for many well-intentioned followers of Jesus who want to pass on their faith to their children. These parents set sail, hoping they're going in the right direction, often depending on life's currents to carry them. They aren't sure how to get where they want to be, and may be relying on misinformation to get there. The result: According to a 2006 survey by the Barna Group (www.barna.org), 61 percent of America's young adults who attended church as teens no longer pray, read the Bible, or go to worship services.

If the story of Christopher Columbus sounds like the way you've been handling the spiritual guidance of your children, you're in good company. Thankfully, it's not too late to do something about it!

Where Are You Going?

In the book *FaithLaunch* (Focus on the Family/Tyndale, 2008), author John Trent describes how he once asked a crowd of parents at a large church three questions.

1. "Do you think it's important to pass down your faith to your children?" As you might expect, more than 90 percent said, "Yes! It's very important!"

2. "Do you think your child will have a strong faith when he or she gets out of college?" Again, 90 percent of those responding said, "You bet!"

3. "Outside of going to church, what are you doing intentionally to introduce and build a growing faith in your child?" Fewer than 30 percent were doing *anything* purposefully to meet that goal during the 166 hours a week their children were at home.

As Trent notes, "Those wonderful, godly, well-intentioned parents strongly believed they should be involved in their children's faith development. They also were highly confident that their children would embrace the faith by the time they were on their own. But when it came to actually preparing their kids, they were just dressing them up and dropping them off at church—and setting themselves up for a failure to launch."

That's where this book comes in. It's not a list of still more things you should be doing for your child or a way to make you feel guiltier than you already do. It's a tool to help you nurture your family's faith in God—in the midst of your real-life, busy days. This is where you'll discover how to develop an intentional, enjoyable spiritual plan for your family—a family covenant—that you can write down and follow all the way to the destination you choose.

But Why a Written Plan?

You've probably heard the saying: "If you fail to plan, you plan to fail." But does that mean you have to put your family covenant to paper, hard drive, or voice recorder? Shouldn't it "just happen"?

In his book *What They Don't Teach You at Harvard Business School* (Bantam, 1986), Mark McCormack describes a study conducted in the 1979 Harvard MBA program. Students were asked, "Have you set clear, written goals for your future and made plans to accomplish them?" Only 3 percent had written goals and plans; 13 percent had unwritten goals; a whopping 84 percent had no specific goals at all. Ten years later the same students were interviewed again. Those who'd had unwritten goals were earning, on average, twice as much as those who'd had no goals at all. The 3 percent who'd written down goals *and* plans were making, on average, *10 times* as much as the other 97 percent put together.

This isn't about income, of course. Far more significant than our ability to earn lots of money is our ability to grow in faith and cultivate our values in the next generation—which takes planning, too.

Written plans aren't exactly alien to most of us. We have "to do" lists, "honey do" lists, grocery lists, plans for vacations and weddings and careers and retirement. Few of us would start building a house without putting pen to paper or hand to computer mouse.

Yet many of us, when it comes to growing in Christ and helping our kids do likewise, tell ourselves that those things will "fall into place" without written plans. Unfortunately, they're more likely to fall apart.

By the time you finish reading this book, you'll be ready to come up with your own customized, *simple* plan—and to get the rest of your family to sign it. But that piece of paper won't be as important as the freedom that will come from knowing where you want to go and how to get there.

You don't have to feel dread about your family's spiritual direction, or suffer under a complicated regimen that tries to turn your living room into a seminary. This book shows how to discover your family's style and strengths, name the things you value, and create a mission statement about where you want to go. You'll identify goals and action steps, and enter into a family covenant to carry them out. Once you know the spiritual truths you want to concentrate on, you can use the teachable moments you have every week to get there.

First Steps

If you're feeling overwhelmed or unsure about how to begin this process, there's good news! Planning your family's spiritual journey won't require a return to the classroom, a school loan, or even a radical change in your schedule. When you're busy, tired, stretched thin—feeling the pressures of life from every angle—you can't take "giant leaps for mankind."

In the 1991 film comedy *What About Bob?* a psychiatrist (Richard Dreyfuss) becomes increasingly frustrated trying to treat a multiphobic patient named Bob Wiley (Bill Murray). The therapist's approach is based on his book, *Baby Steps*. Bob is comforted by the notion that even the most challenging task is manageable if it's broken down into small parts. "Baby steps, baby steps," he mutters throughout the movie.

That's what we need when trying to pass on the faith. Writing a family covenant doesn't have to be a burden. It can unlock the shackles of guilt many of us feel about "never doing enough." As the saying goes, "Inch by inch, everything's a cinch!"

If you've been stifled by feelings of failure when it comes to leading your family spiritually, this book can be a breath of fresh air. No matter what you've tried before, you *can* cultivate your children's faith "when you sit at home and when you walk along the road, when you lie down and when you get up" (Deuteronomy 6:7).

When Your Plan Isn't Perfect

The need for plans doesn't mean, of course, that they'll all pan out. In the words of Proverbs 16:9, "In his heart a man plans his course, but the Lord determines his steps."

We're not infallible, nor immune to making poor decisions that come with tough consequences. Success is in God's hands. If we're willing to depend on Him, though, He'll use our efforts to further His will and work in our families.

And so we plan, knowing that our maps aren't perfect. President Dwight D. Eisenhower, a decorated World War II general who'd plotted and commanded hundreds of critical assaults in theaters of war, put it this way: "In preparing for battle, I have always found that plans are useless, but planning is indispensable."

And We're Off!

Welcome to a journey that's destined to be an adventure you'll never regret—and an exercise your family will never forget.

The stakes are high. This is your chance to chart a course that can affect generations yet to be born.

Even if you're just getting started, congratulations on getting this far in the process. To paraphrase Roman statesman Marcus Cicero, "Beginning is half-done."

So let's go have some fun!

CHAPTER 2

Where Do You Want to End Up?

Kurt and his seven-year-old son, Kyle, piled into the family van. Their destination: McDonald's.

Kurt handed the boy a simple map. "Okay, Kyle. It's up to you to make sure we get to McDonald's." Kurt started the vehicle and proceeded down the street.

At the corner, Kurt stopped and looked over his shoulder. "Where do I go now?"

Kyle looked at the map. "You turn left."

"Naw," Kurt told him. "I think I know what I'm doing; I don't think I need to turn left." He turned right instead.

Kyle burst out in frustration, "It says you're supposed to turn left!"

At the next point of decision, Kurt did the same thing. Soon Kyle was really mad.

When they reached a dead end, Kurt said, "I guess I didn't know where I was going, did I?"

"That's right, Dad, because you were supposed to follow the directions!" Kyle shouted.

"Well, now what are we going to do?" Kurt asked.

"Go back to the beginning and we'll follow the directions."

So they did.

"That's what happens when we don't obey the Bible," Kurt explained as they neared the restaurant. "When we think we know what we're doing and we don't follow the directions, we lose our way. The Scriptures are our directions for life."

Kurt had planned the whole thing, of course. It was a powerful object lesson for Kyle—and a reminder of the importance of knowing where you're going.

Little Pictures, Big Picture

Where would you like your family to be, spiritually speaking, a year from now? Three years? Twenty? What's the ultimate point of planning your family's spiritual direction?

You'll answer that question for yourself later in this book. For now, let's summarize your destination this way: You want to help your children fall in love with Jesus and experience His abundant life.

To do that, you don't have to be incredible. You just have to be intentional.

That isn't going to happen by accident. It will happen because you've decided to begin the process in your own home, to help your children grow up loving the Lord and eventually pass down their faith to their children, your grandchildren.

If that seems like an impossible dream, remember that these things happen a step at a time. Or a snapshot at a time.

Imagine looking at a very large picture of yourself that, as you look more closely, you discover is made up of smaller pictures of all the significant moments in your life. From your birth till now, every experience of your life, every snapshot, has had an impact on you for good or for bad—birthdays, school years, experiences with friends and family. All of those little pictures join together to make up the big picture of who you are today.

The real encouragement for us as parents is that we don't need to spend time worrying about the big picture and how we're going to accomplish this huge task. We just need to concentrate on one little picture at a time and God Himself will take care of the big picture.

How can you intentionally create those individual snapshots in your children's lives? By giving them three things: an unshakable foundation, an internal line, and the big picture.

Target #1: an Unshakable Foundation

What would you think if your real estate agent told you he had a house for you with a foundation *guaranteed* to "never be shaken"? No matter what size earthquake hit your neighborhood, *your* foundation would never move, never shake. If you happened to be moving near a known fault line, you'd have every right to be skeptical.

But God can and did put such a promise in writing. If you read the five verses that make up Psalm 15, you'll see that it's like shooting light through a prism. Those five verses illuminate 10 character traits of a godly person . . . and end with an incredible promise for those who seek to develop them: an unshakable foundation. In King David's words, "He who does these things will never be shaken" (v. 5b).

When you take the time to introduce your children to Jesus and He becomes their personal Lord and Savior, you're laying an unshakable foundation for their lives.

Target #2: an Internal Line

Generations of moviegoers would have lost a hero if it weren't for an unsung hero named William Bachrach. He had a profound impact on a young man named Johnny Weissmuller—who was to become Hollywood's first Tarzan.

When 15-year-old Johnny swam at his "home" pool, he was unbeatable. That pool was one of the finest indoor pools in the country at the time, with thick, black tile stripes marking the lanes that guided the swimmers in competition. While Coach Bachrach and Johnny didn't know it then, those lines were the reason the boy kept losing at away meets.

Subconsciously, Johnny had come to depend on those clearly marked lines to keep him on a straight course. So when he competed in an unmarked pool, his times were dramatically worse.

During an away meet, Bachrach finally figured out the problem. "Johnny!" he roared. "You aren't swimming straight! You don't have that black guideline and so you're wobbling all over the pool!"

To solve the problem, the coach slammed his hat down on a kickboard at one end of the pool and sent Johnny to the other.

"All right now," he ordered, "that hat is your goal. Fix it in your mind, draw a mental line to it, and swim for it." Johnny did, and his times were as fast as ever.

Our children face a similar problem. We do our best to give our children guidelines to follow. In fact, the word for "righteousness" in the Bible means "to stay within the lines."

Our children may thrive when they're in the security of our home where the lines are clear. But outside, they quickly discover that there are no well-marked lines of behavior or commitment. There's nothing to steer children away from problems, stop them from drifting out of bounds, or keep them focused on winning the race when it comes to a godly life.

You can teach your children to stay between the lines of righteous living and to know right from wrong. In so doing, you can keep them pointed toward the positive future God has for them.

Target #3: the Big Picture

When we spiritually train our children, we're preparing them for life, not just for church attendance. This point is further illustrated in Ephesians 6:4: "Fathers, do not exasperate your children; instead, bring them up in the training and instruction of the Lord."

In this one verse Paul sums up or defines what Christian parenting—raising Christian children to adulthood—is.

First of all, we're to "bring them up" in the training and instruction of the Lord. If we're not careful, we may read this as meaning that we should *add* things—like going to church and learning about God, Jesus, and Bible stories—to the overall mix of our children's lives. We then might say something like, "My kids are going to school to get an education, to music lessons to develop their artistic side, and to Sunday school to learn about their faith."

But that's *not* what Paul is saying here. Here's his message: "In every part of bringing them up, in every part of their lives, use the training and instruction of the Lord, teaching them about who they are, what life is about, and how to live according to God's principles and His Word."

Spiritual training is not an add-on; it forms the core of your children's being and life. If we imagine our children's large pictures made up of all those little pictures, their spiritual training should be the foundation of, and the reason for, the orderly placement of every one of those images.

That sounds like a tall order—until we remember that it's one little picture at a time.

First Things First

For many parents, the notion of doing "spiritual stuff" at home creates a knot of tension in the stomach due to past failure or intimidation.

Let's start with a clean sheet of paper. Erase all your preconceived notions about training your children in the Christian faith. For a moment forget all the guilt-driven, unpleasant attempts you've made in the past or any ideas you may have about this being boring and ineffective.

There are four principles that can ensure that your efforts aren't in vain. Remembering them can keep the process simple and your priorities clear.

Principle #1: Relationship Is Your Priority

Kathleen grew up in a Christian home. She attended church regularly with Mom, Dad, and her siblings. The family Bible was prominently displayed on the den coffee table. There was prayer before every meal, even in restaurants. But there was one problem: Kathleen and her father, a successful professional who worked long hours and traveled a lot, didn't get along.

During childhood, Kathleen barely got to know her dad. By the time she was a junior in high school, the tension between her and her father was thick. Whenever he led the family in prayer or tried to read a short devotion, her body stiffened. As the family marched dutifully into church behind her deacon father, Kathleen felt sick to her stomach. In those moments every fault in his life was magnified and profound disrespect burned in her heart.

When Kathleen left home as a young adult, she left the faith of her family as well.

There are countless Kathleens in the world. The old adage is true—people don't care how much you know until they know how much you care. If we want the values we teach our children to stick, we must apply heavy amounts of the glue called love.

Principle #2: The Bible Is Your Handbook

God gave us an instruction manual for life—the Bible. Asking, "Should I be teaching my children the Bible or should I wait until they're old enough to decide for themselves?" is like asking, "Should I make my children eat fruits and vegetables and have a proper diet now, or should I let them eat what they want until they're old enough to decide for themselves?"

The Bible is "useful for teaching, rebuking, correcting and training in righteousness" (2 Timothy 3:16). It's our guidebook, lifeline, textbook, help menu, answer, emergency first aid kit—and, most importantly, our key to knowing God.

Principle #3: Life Is Your Classroom

No one becomes great at what he does through classroom instruction alone. Would you care how many books the surgeon who's about to take out your gall bladder has read if you knew that was the total of his training? On the other hand, you'd be equally scared of a surgeon who'd never read any books about the human body or the techniques of surgery but was on his second operation and "doing much better."

God has designed the world and us so that learning about spiritual things and applying them in everyday life happen together. That's the idea behind Deuteronomy 6:6-9. We're to impress God's commands on our children daily. We're to talk about them when we sit at home, when we're on the road, when we lie down at night, and when we get up in the morning. This can't be accomplished merely by taking our children to church and reading them Bible stories. We need to demonstrate to them—through our growth, by our example, and by when and what we teach—that our faith is about who we are, how we act, and what we do as well as about what we believe.

Practice-what-you-preach parenting is the only kind that works. But parenting by example doesn't demand that we be perfect.

We're all fellow learners. Our children and we are both learning about God. This means discussing our growth in Christ in practical, everyday terms with them. It includes letting them see us apply our faith to our lives. Then they'll get excited about joining the process. It's easier to get kids in the water when you're swimming than when you're sitting warm and dry on the beach.

Principle #4: Adapting to Your Child Is Important

We can't expect children to rise to our level; we need to go to theirs. When Jesus said, "Let the little children come to me" (Mark 10:14), He stopped doing what He was doing to communicate truth to adults and adapted His approach for a new audience.

Mark 10:16 says, "And he took the children in his arms, put his hands on them and blessed them." Jesus changed what He was doing in order to be effective with the children.

We need to be able to understand what the important issues are for our children—in their eyes, not ours—and communicate on their level. When we can at least imagine walking in their shoes, our teaching will be more effective and relevant.

Where You're Going

Maybe you have questions, hesitations, and fears about coming up with a family covenant. But you can become intentional about passing on your faith and values—and have a great time doing it!

The first step is to really understand your family. That's what the next chapter is about.

 POINT • OF • ACTION

What preconceived notions do you need to erase in order to get started on a family covenant? Write five words on a sheet of paper that describe any spiritual training you may have received when you were growing up. Then write five words that describe any fears or doubts about your ability to create or carry out a plan.

Now cross out any negative words on your first list, keeping in mind that you don't have to duplicate mistakes that may have been made in your own spiritual training. Then read the "Troubleshooting" section at the end of this book. How does it apply to your second list?

CHAPTER 3

What Are You and Your Family Like?

It's been said that families are a lot like fudge—mostly sweet, with a few nuts mixed in for good measure.

The Addams Family was one such clan. This popular television comedy was based on the creation of cartoonist Charles Addams, whose work first appeared as single panels in *The New Yorker* magazine in the 1930s. It featured the antics of an eccentric, bizarre family whose members thought they were the "normal" ones—and that everyone *else* was strange!

Patriarch Gomez and wife, Morticia, along with crazy Uncle Fester, seemed to meander through life, guiding children Wednesday and Pugsley accidentally, if at all. Viewers were never sure how or why the family had grown so odd. A peek into the past would have been revealing—but might have ruined half the fun.

The Addamses were a motley bunch, and certainly in need of a plan for properly shepherding their kids. Your family might not be as eccentric, but chances are you have plenty of quirks, too.

Fortunately, there's no such thing as a "typical" family. And there's no "typical" way in which to pass on your faith to your children.

Since your faith is expressed through the one-of-a-kind life your family leads, your covenant should match who you are. What will work for someone else's family may not work for yours at all. That's why you need to "paint some portraits" of your unique family before you begin.

Family Portrait #1: Your History of Faith

We are, like it or not, a product of the lives that have touched ours.

Sol Tax, a professor of anthropology at the University of Chicago, was carrying his granddaughter on his shoulders one day. They happened to cross paths with a friend who hadn't seen the little girl for almost a year.

"My, how you've grown!" the acquaintance said.

She quickly responded, "Well, you know, not all of this is me!"

Not all of what we are today is our own doing. It's often helpful to pause and consider where we've come from and remember on whose shoulders we sit. "The farther backward you can look," said Sir Winston Churchill, "the farther forward you are likely to see."

Some of us are glad our pasts are behind us; others wax nostalgic for days gone by. Either way, it's a good idea to take inventory of your family's spiritual history.

Try sitting down with your loved ones, grabbing some paper and a pen, and taking a stroll down memory lane. Dr. Neill Q. Hamilton, author of *Maturing in the Christian Life* (Geneva Press, 1984), suggests using questions like these:

> 1. Were your parents Christians? In what ways did they influence and inspire your faith formation as you were growing up?

2. Were there other adults who had an important influence on your religious nurture? Who were they and what influence did they have?

3. In your adult years, what ministers, friends, teachers, or authors have had a special hand in shaping the faith you now hold? What were their contributions, both positive and negative?

4. Was there a time when you consciously decided to become a Christian? What were the circumstances? Did any particular experiences of God lead up to or accompany this?

Of course, this isn't a comprehensive analysis of your spiritual heritage. But it's a start. And best of all, there are no wrong answers. It's your family's story.

Another aspect of your history is your status as a first-, second-, or third-generation Christian.

Jim and Deborah are both first-generation Christians. Neither grew up in a home with a strong commitment to Christ. Jim darkened the door of a church with about the same frequency as the Chicago Cubs win the World Series. Deborah had a bit more exposure to church, but never heard what it means to have a personal relationship with Jesus Christ. Both became Christians in high school.

First-generation Christians have hurdles to clear, with no tangible models of faith to follow. But they bring advantages to the table—including their zeal and ability to tailor their spiritual strategies without any "But that's not the way we did it" problem.

Second-generation Christians grew up in a household of faith, often going to church regularly and maybe having family devotions. There are advantages to this background: some Bible knowledge and perhaps a personal history with God. Yet many second-generation Christians struggle to cultivate a burning passion for Christ, taking their faith for granted. If parents lose their passion and neglect their calling to spiritually train their children, the children often walk away. If this is you, ask God to help you get your spark back so you can start a fire of faith in your kids.

Third-generation Christians often have the example of two or more generations before them who loved and followed the Lord. Those who hail from such stock are ahead of the game. Those whose Christian ancestors were more inconsistent or too passive in conveying their faith may face a greater—but not insurmountable—challenge.

If you and your spouse have different backgrounds—for example, if you're a first-generation Christian and your spouse is a third-generation—use your differing strengths to your advantage when planning your personal and family journeys.

Family Portrait #2: Your Pace

Knowing your "speed" will help you come up with action steps that fit your family.

1. *The Carriage Family.* Donna and Jim are nothing if not laid-back. They ambled through college and finished their three-year courses in four years. They stroll through life enjoying things, nature, and people. They operate at a lower stress level because the clock doesn't tyrannize them. "Life is too short," Jim would say.

The Carriage Family has the time and often the setting to put in place a wonderful family covenant. These households are also usually good at starting slowly and spending time. Sometimes they resist change, though—especially adding structure.

2. *The Steam Engine Family.* Remember the "little engine that could"? It kept chugging along until it saved the day. That's Ron and Julie Smith. Their Steam Engine Family is characterized by steadiness, consistency . . . and increasing commitments. They keep adding responsibilities, plotting their schedule on a large calendar with lots of room to write.

The Steam Engine Family, once convinced that the spiritual training of children is important, will be quick to add that boxcar to the train. If this is you, your tendency to put a full-blown plan in place immediately may lead to burnout. Try starting with a very basic plan; you can add boxcars later if you wish.

3. *The F-16 Family.* Jim and Tanya met, fell in love, and were married in less than four months. Activity is their hallmark. Between work, church, and kids' programs, they can't miss two stoplights in the morning without running behind.

F-16 Families struggle to find time to teach systematically. Boredom can come easily, consistency is a challenge, and getting the family together is a rarity. If this is you, concentrate on redeeming the time you're already spending—such as drive times, those occasional meals together, and bedtimes.

No matter which family pace best describes your situation, make sure that as you develop your covenant, you consider your speed without trying to change it. If you're currently running at a pace that isn't right for your family, treat that as a separate issue. Using your plan to accomplish a pace change could cause your family to resent the plan.

Family Portrait #3: Your Interests

When you channel-surf the networks, where do you end up? Nature shows? Baseball games? Classic movies? Believe it or not, the answer can significantly affect your family covenant. The more passionate you are about something, the more time, energy, and effort you'll put into doing that thing and doing it well. What excites your family is an open door to their hearts, and connecting your covenant to that gives you a huge head-start!

Here are some examples of the "channels" your family might frequent.

1. *The Discovery Network.* Does your family love science, animals, and creation? Do you camp and go for hikes to get close to nature? Use that love to teach about the Lord. Focus on Bible stories about creation, nature, and God's power and creativity. Go to zoos, wildlife sanctuaries, or science fairs. Go for hikes and explain how nature points to God. Use metaphors such as sin being like a snake's bite that can poison your whole system.

2. *The Sports Network.* If your family is interested in sports, use that to make learning spiritual things relevant and fun. Discover the stories of athletes or heroes in the Bible. Find books on Christian sports stars. Send your kids to Christian sports camps. Play sports together and relate them to the Christian life. Your family probably will want its covenant oriented toward activities, not theorizing.

3. *The Arts Network.* Do you have budding Da Vincis under your roof? Will the next Pavarotti or Elvis spring from your den? Link your family with artists who match the talent God gave them with love for Jesus. Introduce them to artists of the past who excelled and credited God. Go to museums, plays, and art galleries, and then discuss how they display biblical principles (or not). Get your family involved in your church's music or drama. Find ways to explain spiritual principles through intuition, images, stories, pictures, patterns, and designs—not just logic.

4. *The Biography Network.* Is your family people-oriented? Are you "social butterflies" or "party animals"? If you're a biography family, focus on Bible characters and what they did, how they followed God, why they made right (or wrong) choices. Use stories of Christians who were scientists, heroes, or martyrs. Invite missionaries, pastors, and visiting speakers to your home. Help the needy through your church's outreach programs. Throw parties to mark spiritual milestones. Relate what you're studying to your children's interactions with friends.

The list of possible "networks" is endless. The point is not to bore your kids, but to get them excited.

Family Portrait #4: Your Strengths and Values

What's your family good at? Here's a quiz to help you answer that question. Which of the following has your family tried—and liked enough to want to try again?
- having people over for a party
- letting a non-family member live in your home for at least a week
- visiting a nursing home, hospital, or shut-in
- singing or playing musical instruments together
- participating in a political campaign or protest
- camping, hiking, or rock climbing
- putting on a play
- helping with vacation Bible school or a missions trip
- playing faithfully in a sports league
- raising money for a project
- building a tree house or Christmas light display

- starting a business
- other _____

What strengths are reflected in your answers? Does your family have a knack for hospitality, performing, organizing, competing, traveling, earning, giving, taking a stand, or heavy lifting?

When it came to strengths, the Gardners were a mixed bag. Mom and son excelled at making things. Dad was good at meeting people. So they put together sacks of homemade cookies and candy, then went from bed to bed in a nursing home and handed out treats and conversation. The family used its strengths to serve—sending a lasting message to the son about the importance and fulfillment of serving in Christ's name.

Family strengths often spring from values. The Pavlovs cherish their eastern European heritage and love children, which explains why they're so good at visiting Russian orphanages in the summer. The Lopez family prizes personal responsibility; it's no surprise that others count on them to show up for every soccer drill and worship team meeting.

What are your family's values? Which of the following qualities do you most hope to see in your children as they grow?

- loyalty
- perseverance
- generosity
- compassion
- leadership
- humility
- discernment
- self-control
- friendliness

• objectivity
• patience

That's only a partial list, of course. You can take inventory of your own values as you consider a "mission statement" for your family in the next chapter.

When in Doubt, Adapt

Use what you learn about your family to create a covenant that fits. You may find you're like author Dr. Timothy Keller, senior pastor of Redeemer Presbyterian Church in New York City. He once said that every family Bible study he tried to start with his wife and three boys failed miserably! So he decided to improvise. After prayer and thought, he established the habit of taking each child out for a one-on-one meal each week. There they'd discuss the things they *would* have talked about during their study of the Scriptures.

There was something very intimate about eating a meal together, he said, that got his kids to open up in conversation. By considering the unique characteristics and qualities of his family, Keller was able to begin designing its spiritual training. And for his family, it worked.

Families that pursue a relationship with Jesus Christ may not be all alike, but their spiritual courses point in the same direction. They just need to proceed at their own pace, with their own style, and building on their own strengths.

 POINT • OF • ACTION

What are your family's top four or five values? To answer that question, it may be helpful to think through some life-changing experiences your family has undergone. For example, the stress of a car accident or long illness might have helped you realize how important the value of peace is to you.

Once you've listed your most strongly held values, write them in the "Values" section of the worksheet at the end of this book.

CHAPTER 4

Making Your Plan: Mission, Goals, and Action Steps

We're about to cross from theory to nuts-and-bolts reality. We've considered the importance of guiding our families spiritually; we've analyzed our pasts and presents. We've looked ahead and begun to dream of who our children might someday be.

There's a problem, though. It might be summed up this way:

1. The road to you-know-where is paved with good intentions.

2. The best-laid plans of mice and men often go astray.

3. Dreamers aren't usually doers.

It's one thing to identify a need—but another to do something about it.

So let's do something!

Your Mission

First, it's time to draft a mission statement that captures God's unique calling for you and your family. As God instructed the prophet

Habakkuk: "Write down the revelation and make it plain on tablets so that a herald may run with it" (Habakkuk 2:2).

A spiritual family mission statement proclaims what your family believes God wants you to accomplish. It doesn't need to be flowery or formal. In fact, it's best to keep it so simple that everyone can understand it. Consider these mission statements guiding the leadership of some well-known companies:

Wal-Mart: *Saving people money so they can live better.*

Canon: *To contribute to global prosperity and the well-being of humankind.*

Ford Motor Company: *To become the world's leading consumer company for automotive products and services.*

A family mission statement might look something like these:

We want to be the kind of family whose love for each other attracts our neighbors to follow Jesus.

To help suffering people in other countries have enough to eat, drink, and wear, and to let them know that we're doing it in Jesus' name.

Our family finds out what the Bible says and obeys it, even if it costs us money and friends.

Your mission, of course, may vary.

So how do you go about writing a family mission statement? Here are a few tips:

1. *Ask for God's help.* He promises to give us wisdom if we request it (James 1:5-8). If you want to see some examples of mission statements in His Word, check out Genesis 18:19, Joshua 24:15, and Philippians 1:21.

2. *Identify your core values.* What's truly important to your family? Are you especially concerned about evangelism? The homeless? Frugality? Worshiping God through the arts? Many values are vital,

but choosing two or three you care most about will help make your mission statement specific enough to write goals for.

3. *Involve the kids.* Have a meeting and ask *them* what they believe God wants your family to do. You have veto power, but take the input seriously.

4. *Don't rush.* Mission statements should be short, but that doesn't mean creating them is quick. It takes time to think through what your family is really about, and to boil that down to its essentials. Avoid settling for a generic "To glorify God" or "To serve humanity."

5. *Make your statement succinct and memorable.* "To explore strange, new worlds, to seek out new life and new civilizations, to boldly go where no man has gone before." Now there's a mission statement that's hard to misunderstand or forget! Ask yourself whether every member of your family over age three or so will be able to grasp and remember your mission.

6. *Agree as parents before asking kids to ratify the result.* If you have a spouse, discuss and refine your statement together before calling another family meeting. Lingering doubts from the grown-ups may unnecessarily prolong the process.

7. *Keep your statement before you.* Don't just file it away or leave it on your computer. Post it in a prominent place. Some families even print theirs on "business" cards that family members can carry with them as reminders.

Your Goals

It was the first day of community college, and the astronomy teacher was trying to size up the caliber of his class. "What do you hope to get out of this semester?" he asked one of the students.

"Four credits," came the reply.

Everyone laughed but the instructor. "If that's all you're here for," he said, "that's all you'll get. I'd encourage you to set some goals for yourself. Goals will help keep the train on the tracks."

Goals flow from your mission. You can't fulfill your purpose without them. Mission statements may last a lifetime; goals are measurable, time-sensitive, specific targets.

Some examples:

We will spend 10 minutes a week praying together.
We will memorize the books of the Bible by November 15.
We will host a backyard VBS at our home this summer.

Does it really help to name and write down goals? The Flaherty family discovered that it does. The parents decided to work with their two boys, ages four and six, on becoming more loving. Peter, the father, was trying to get the younger boy dressed for church one day when the older son expressed disgust over having to wait. "Come on, Dad!" he said. "We're going to be late!"

"Sean," Peter muttered, "we're working on patience."

The boy frowned. "Dad, I thought we were working on *love*!"

Peter smiles now when he tells that story. It's a pleasant surprise to find that your kids were listening when you gave them an assignment. Sean remembered the goal because it was specific—and agreed upon. Your family can do the same.

Three Sample Family Plans

What should your goals look like?

Once upon a time there were three very different (and fictional) families. Each had varying needs and children of various ages, but all had the same commitment—to see each family member grow in Christ. Let's look at how they approached their first family covenants.

Family #1: The Bilbys

The Bilbys are a blended family with a 16-year-old, two six-year-old twin boys, and a mile-a-minute two-year-old. They decided they were an F-16 Family. They'd been praying and talking about teaching their children about the Lord at home, but had some difficulty agreeing on what to do.

The Bilby family was a zoo when it came to personality types. Family interests ranged from fiction to the Sports Channel.

Mike and Raye Ann set goals. They'd begin to sprinkle their family fun with spiritual content, using videos, board games, and Christian fiction. They decided that the most important on-the-go training they could do was to take time to answer their children's questions about God.

Next they had a family meeting and discussed the importance of having a covenant. They chose a book of "family night" activities, and family members took on responsibilities like rounding up participants, gathering materials, preparing snacks, and making sure everyone understood the main point of the lesson.

Mike also liked the idea of using driving time, and planned to start leading learning games in the car. Looking to connect with their teenage daughter in her last two years before college, Mike and Raye Ann would take her through a topical study once a week.

Their family covenant ended up looking like this:

- Once a week: Attend church as a family.
- Once every other Tuesday night: Do a family activity that makes a spiritual point.

- Once a day, Monday through Friday: Spend 10 minutes with the twins at night, reading a Bible story or "bedtime blessing" and praying with them individually.
- Once a day, Monday through Friday: Spend 15 minutes reading the Bible or a devotional book with the 16-year-old and praying with her.

Family #2: The Wootenbergs

Marsha Wootenberg is a single mom with two daughters, ages eight and eleven. She identified her threesome as a Steam Engine Family. As a single, working parent she was careful not to over-commit—and agreed to follow a family covenant "for three months only."

Since Marsha had always made an effort to sit down as a family and talk at mealtimes, she and her kids decided mealtimes would be when they did their family time. She kept it short, reading through a devotion and leading the activity accompanying it.

Marsha and her girls set goals together. Because they were all relatively new to the Christian faith, the girls told their mom that they wanted to go to the new believers' class at church with her. After discussing the need for personal time with God, the older daughter decided to use a devotional book that some of the other kids her age were using. The younger daughter wanted to read Bible stories and begin to pray with her mom before bed.

Marsha's first covenant was simple:

- Once a week: Attend church (three times a month due to her work schedule).
- Once every other Thursday night: Do a family activity that teaches a lesson.
- Once a day, in the morning: Pray for the children.

Family #3: The Bannisters

Kevin and Cindy Bannister had a typical SITCOM family (Single Income, Three Children, Oppressive Mortgage). They had two sons, ages five and seven, and a three-year-old daughter. Kevin and Cindy were also strong Christians with a deep desire to communicate their faith to their children.

The Bannisters had moved to a part of the country that was at a polar extreme to their Bible Belt upbringing. At first they felt cut off and alone when it came to their faith. In a way that was good; they realized how much of their children's spiritual growth they'd "out-sourced" to their former church.

They'd been an F-16 Family before, but moved at more of a Carriage pace now that Cindy was home with the kids. They decided they could raise the bar a bit on the basic family covenant.

The Bannisters picked a small church with a decent children's program. Then they set an evening aside, after the kids were in bed, to put together their plan.

One of their goals was to support each other in getting their own daily time with God back on track. Kevin also liked the idea of giving the kids the "big story" of the Bible. Toward that end, he found some good audio tapes and planned to play them for the kids whenever they were in the car together.

Since all their children were "Bible-story age," they decided to sit down together as a family before bed and read. Here was the rest of their agreement:

- Once a week: Attend church.
- Once a week, usually Wednesday night: Do a spiritual training time with each child.
- Once every other Friday: Have a family activity night.
- Once a day at bedtime: Pray for each child.

Finding a support group was a challenge. They told Cindy's parents about their plan; her parents were excited and offered to help by praying and including Christian videos, games, magazines, software, and picture books among the Christmas and birthday presents they sent.

Action Steps

Even the most profound mission statement and loftiest goals will come to naught if you don't add action steps.

Action steps are the "to do" list of family covenants. Here's how one family followed through on its goal "to be intentional about modeling faith at home":

Action step 1: At the dinner table, have the "Best and Worst" conversation to find teachable moments. ("What was the best part of your day? What was the worst?")

Action step 2: Pray every day as a family for each other and for our community.

Action step 3: As a family, serve at the local mission to help the homeless. Make it a tradition to always serve at Thanksgiving and Christmas.

The same family members also had the goal to "reach out to our community." These action steps were designed to get them there:

Action step 1: Actively pursue families and individuals who don't seem connected to the community.

Action step 2: Model unconditional love, regardless of belief, culture, or spiritual status.

Action step 3: Lead a small group in our neighborhood.

Don't forget to attach action steps to each of your goals. After all, you want to be intentional—not just full of good intentions.

Sounds Like a Plan

Now it's your turn. After reviewing your family information, start putting together your covenant.

What's your mission? What are your goals? The action steps you want to take? Be as detailed as you want to be.

Move from your family's characteristics to your family's activities. Note what you're already doing that falls under the umbrella of spiritual training.

As you plan, remember that God wants to give you time to grow as well. For example, you may need an hour during the week by yourself to pray, study the Bible in more depth, or just sit quietly in God's presence. Or you may need to find support in a small group. Meeting your own spiritual needs is part of your responsibility in training your children.

If yours is a two-parent family, discuss your plans and encourage each other to stick with them. Have a family meeting to get the input of your kids. Listen to everyone's ideas; be willing to modify the plan.

Emphasize that the details of the covenant are not set in stone. Choose a time when you'll all review it to see if it's working and, if necessary, to improve it.

After committing yourselves by signing the plan as a covenant (see Chapter 5), post it in a prominent place—perhaps on the refrigerator. You might even want to frame it.

Then celebrate! And remember to undergird your family and its spiritual growth each day with prayer.

 ## POINT • OF • ACTION

With your family's help, draft a mission statement that's Christ-centered, action-oriented, and legacy-driven. Write it in the "Mission" portion of the worksheet at the end of this book.

Then write three to five goals for spiritual development, aiming to fulfill them by this time next year. Make sure they're consistent with your overall mission and values. Write your goals in the "Goals" part of the worksheet.

Finally, write one or two action steps for each goal and add these to the "Action Steps" portion of the worksheet.

CHAPTER 5

A Covenant You Can Keep

"Good fences," wrote poet Robert Frost, "make good neighbors."

Sometimes, though, they're not enough.

Take, for instance, the eccentric doctor in Mission Viejo, California, who constructed a model volcano in his backyard. Neighbors filed a lawsuit because the shooting flames blocked their views of a golf course.

Nearby, another homeowner wound up in court after he tried to run a full-sized steam locomotive on 500 feet of track—in his backyard.

And then there was old Ragtime, a miniature horse who liked to sit on the couch and eat popcorn with her owners—in full view of passersby. When crowds began to gather, neighbors sued to send Ragtime out to pasture—or at least off the couch and out of the spotlight.

Fences don't solve problems like those. Far more effective are written agreements among homeowners, otherwise known as *covenants*.

The Whats and Whys of Covenants

According to the tenth edition of *Merriam-Webster's Collegiate Dictionary*, a covenant is a "formal, solemn, and binding agreement . . .

a written agreement or promise usually under seal between two or more parties especially for the performance of some action."

In theological terms, covenants were created by God as a way to confirm His agreements with mankind. In biblical terms, the word "covenant" is interchangeable with "agreement," but carries far more weight than a casual or even contractual understanding.

Here are six traits of these spiritual agreements found in the Bible:

1. *They bring safety.* Without the following agreement, Noah and his family and all the animals would have perished: "'But I will establish my covenant with you, and you will enter the ark—you and your sons and your wife and your sons' wives with you. You are to bring into the ark two of all living creatures, male and female, to keep them alive with you. . . .' Noah did everything just as God commanded him" (Genesis 6:18-19, 22).

2. *They have an outward sign.* These can be important, reminding the parties of their agreement and helping others to hold them accountable. Examples: wedding rings and written family covenants. "And God said, 'This is the sign of the covenant I am making between me and you and every living creature with you, a covenant for all generations to come: I have set my rainbow in the clouds, and it will be the sign of the covenant between me and the earth'" (Genesis 9:12-13).

3. *They can focus on one or more generations.* Living our agreements and modeling them to our children can help future generations live out their own. "On that day the LORD made a covenant with Abram and said, 'To your descendants I give this land, from the river of Egypt to the great river, the Euphrates—the land of the Kenites, Kenizzites, Kadmonites, Hittites, Perizzites, Rephaites, Amorites, Canaanites, Girgashites and Jebusites'" (Genesis 15:18-21).

4. *They can multiply productivity.* People accomplish more when God is on the team. "'I will confirm my covenant between me and you and will greatly increase your numbers'" (Genesis 17:2).

5. *They bring a new identity.* When you enter into a covenant, you become a part of a bigger story. "'No longer will you be called Abram; your name will be Abraham, for I have made you a father of many nations. I will make you very fruitful; I will make nations of you, and kings will come from you'" (Genesis 17:5-6).

6. *They require sacrifice.* Most contracts protect your rights and limit your responsibilities. Most spiritual covenants call on you to give up your rights and take on responsibilities. "'This is my covenant with you and your descendants after you, the covenant you are to keep: Every male among you shall be circumcised'" (Genesis 17:10).

Covenants are powerful. They help us achieve what we often struggle to do on our own. When two parties come together with a common goal, strengths are combined, weaknesses are minimized, and the chances of success are exponentially increased.

Your Family Covenant

In this book we've been walking our way through why it's so important to have a family covenant. You're probably convinced that you *need* and *want* to do it, and know *how* to do it. But sometimes, like fences, good intentions just aren't enough.

Why? Well, think about the last few months. Have you been busy? Were there unexpected interruptions—perhaps sick children, backlogged e-mail, nagging headaches, unfinished home projects, assignments at work, last-minute church meetings, soccer games, music lessons, dentist appointments? Do you honestly think it will be much different during the next few months? How about the next year?

Reducing your pace is probably a good idea, but that's a topic for another time. For now, let's assume there's nothing on the horizon that will magically take away all the activity or give you a 32-hour day. So it's not a matter of when you will have the time, but *whether you will commit yourself to the process.*

That involves sacrifice. Sacrifice is not the easiest word to swallow. Most of us prefer having our rights protected, not giving something up or surrendering our independence. But as Paul told the believers at Corinth, "Nobody should seek his own good, but the good of others" (1 Corinthians 10:24). To those at Philippi he wrote, "Each of you should look not only to your own interests, but also to the interests of others" (Philippians 2:4). When we enter a covenant relationship, we're surrendering our personal desires and putting the needs of our families first.

As parents, the most important agreement we can make is to accept God's grace. This allows and motivates us to make healthy covenants with those around us. We can freely surrender in these other spiritual agreements, knowing that Christ has agreed to be our protector, our provider, and ever-present help.

Two Families' Covenants

Are you ready to put pen to paper and draft your family covenant if you haven't done so already? Need some ideas? Here's the agreement one family signed:

Smith Family Covenant

Mission: To experience the unconditional love of Christ, so we might love one another and make a radical impact on our family, community, and culture.

Values: Unconditional love, healthy and safe environment, quality time (just being, not doing), honesty, friends, community, food, fun

Goal 1: To be intentional about modeling our faith at home.

Goal 2: To reach out to our community.

We as a family agree with God to fulfill the above, by the means discussed in Ephesians 3:14-21.

Bob Smith   Carly Smith   Megan Smith   Chad Smith

Want another example? Here's the simple, straightforward plan another family agreed to.

Jones Family Covenant

Mission: We will love, encourage, and serve one another and those God brings into our lives.

Values: Love, peace, fun, family relationships, trust

Goals: (1) To memorize 12 Bible verses about God's love in the coming year; and (2) to tangibly express God's love through service

Action steps: (1) Memorize one verse about love each month in the coming year; and (2) express God's love through a service opportunity that we do as a family.

Nat Jones   Tyra Jones   Connor Jones   Kylie Jones

Your family's covenant doesn't have to look exactly like either of those. But what would it look like to have your relationships renewed and motivated by God's grace? How would your children respond if you were a servant leader like Christ? A written covenant can make clear what that means in your family, and cement your commitment to make it happen no matter how busy your days continue to be.

 POINT • OF • ACTION

If you haven't done so already, write your family covenant—including values, mission, goals, and action steps—on the worksheet in the back of this book. Print the final version, frame it if desired, and have all family members sign it. Post this spiritual agreement prominently in your home.

Celebrate the signing of this document. Set a date, perhaps six months or a year from now, when you'll celebrate your progress and adjust the covenant if needed.

Share your covenant with a support group—Sunday school class, church small group, friends—so that those walking with you can help you fulfill your plan.

CHAPTER 6

Tools You Can Use

The town of Leadville, Colorado, perches at just over 10,000 feet above sea level in the heart of the Rocky Mountains. Each August, runners from all over the world gather there for a grueling 100-mile race—the Leadville Trail 100.

Participants gather in the pre-dawn dark to receive final instructions along with a pep talk from the race's founder, Ken Chlouber. Afterward, many find his few words to be the reason they didn't quit when the going got tough.

"You're better than you think you are," he tells the participants every year, "and you can do more than you think you can."

The same can be said for you, if you're committed to passing on the Christian faith to your children. It's actually far easier than you might realize to stay on course in following your family covenant.

For one thing, you're probably already engaged in activities that help foster, nurture, and transfer your beliefs and values. A few slight adjustments might be enough. And even if they're not, more extensive changes don't have to be jarring or unpleasant.

Let's consider some methods you can use to carry out your covenant. The more varied and enjoyable your methods are, the more likely it is that you'll stay on course.

Church Activities

The best support for your spiritual training efforts is usually your local church. Get involved in the programs offered—worship services, Sunday school, vacation Bible school, youth groups, Bible clubs.

When we consistently demonstrate the priority of attending worship, our children learn to place a high priority there as well. An additional benefit: Kids are more likely to consistently meet and make good friends in a church than on a playground.

Mealtime, Drive Time, Bedtime

Here are three times you can use for fun and effective spiritual training.

1. *Mealtime.* Everybody has to eat! Take advantage of time spent dining together by discussing spiritual topics in an enjoyable, unforced way. By doing this, you help your children overcome the notion that spirituality is just a "church thing."

Creative questioning at mealtime is a good way to avoid boring children with doctrinal discussions. Posing queries like, "Did anyone see the beautiful sunset this evening?" can elicit comments about the beauty of God's creation. Talking about a friend who just recovered from a serious illness gives you an opportunity to discuss the Lord's healing powers. However you go about it, keep these things in mind: Personalize it; time it right; keep it short; keep it relevant.

2. *Drive time.* Between school, doctor visits, grocery shopping, music lessons, and athletic contests, you may spend hours each week in a vehicle with your children. Redeem some of that time by using it to convey spiritual truth, fulfilling the modern-day equivalent of teaching "when you walk along the road" (Deuteronomy 6:7). Topics could be an extension or continuation of mealtime conversations.

Keep it simple, make it fun, and take advantage of those periods when children tend to be talkative and energetic.

3. *Bedtime.* Many families already have a bedtime routine. These can be ideal opportunities for spiritual training, affirmation of love, and prayer. Bedtime activities provide high value for the time spent. If you're willing to make the effort, your relationship with your child—and with God—will be reinforced.

Teachable Moments

One of the easiest ways to guide children spiritually is to use teachable moments. These are times when you're with your child and something happens that offers an opportunity to tell him or her about God. It's as simple as paying attention to the world around you and presenting it from a godly viewpoint. After all, the most effective learning takes place in the context of real life.

You may not be able to manufacture moments, but you won't have to if you're alert. Let's say you've been undercharged at the supermarket; you can discuss why you need to go back and pay the clerk the difference. Take your kids with you, let them listen to the conversation, and talk about it on the way home.

Or perhaps someone in a parking lot has a flat tire; you can help him or her change it. Watching is powerful for children—probably more so than talking. Be on the lookout for chances to model the Christian life.

Setting an example is important because children learn from us whether we're trying to teach them or not. Consider Hank, age two and a half. Ever since he was born, his parents had prayed openly—though not formally—in his presence. When the phone rang one day, his mother answered it while he played with his trains on the living room floor. When she hung up, Hank asked whom she'd been speaking with. "I was talking with Grandpa," she told him. "Grandma broke her hip and is in the hospital."

"Oh," Hank replied. "Mommy, we need to pray for her right now!"

Whether they meant to or not, Hank's parents had taught him the importance of prayer. Values like that are caught during teachable moments.

Family Devotions

Family Bible study is an opportunity to stop and reflect together on a passage of Scripture. It can be very positive if done effectively—especially by relating God's Word to a child's everyday needs. There's no right or wrong way to conduct family devotions, but the following might serve as a guideline:

1. Read a Scripture passage first.

2. Read a devotional story or a section of a family devotional book.

3. Ask questions based on the two readings. Strive to be uplifting and encouraging; don't lecture or squelch answers.

4. Pray together. You might "go around the circle" and have everyone contribute a suggestion or two on what to pray for. Review past prayer requests and update the family on how things are going. Some families fasten a small whiteboard on the refrigerator, listing the top three items to pray for as a reminder throughout the week.

Keys to success with family devotions include taking it slowly, sharing the responsibility, letting kids offer input, setting a time limit, keeping things simple, and encouraging discussion. Some parents have found one-on-one time at a restaurant easier to manage than an organized study; try to remain flexible and sensitive to the changing needs and interests of your child.

Family Nights

Is it possible to drive home a spiritual truth and have fun at the same time? Family nights are a great way to do just that. Try setting aside an evening for creative activities and object lessons that make a point. When children enjoy time with their parents, they're far more motivated to embrace the values and beliefs we hope to teach them.

Here's an example:

There's toothpaste all over the plastic-covered table. Four young children are having the time of their lives squeezing the paste out of four tubes—trying to get every last bit out of them as Dad has told them to.

"Okay," says Dad, slapping a $20 bill onto the table. "The first person to get the toothpaste back into the tube gets this money!" Little hands begin working to shove the peppermint-flavored goo back into the rolled-up tubes, but almost none makes it back through the narrow opening.

"We can't do it, Dad!" protests the youngest child.

"Ah, that's just like your tongue," says Dad. "Once the words come out, it's impossible to get them back in. You need to be careful what you say because you may wish you could take it back, but you can't. That's why the Bible says we must watch our tongue."

Family nights are an entertaining tool for teaching profound truths. Which do you think your child is more likely to remember:

a straightforward reading of the following verses from James, or one reinforced with toothpaste?

> My dear brothers, take note of this: Everyone should be quick to listen, slow to speak and slow to become angry, for man's anger does not bring about the righteous life that God desires. . . . If anyone considers himself religious and yet does not keep a tight rein on his tongue, he deceives himself and his religion is worthless. (James 1:19-20, 26)

Eyes on the Prize

Charlie Brown, the beloved but wishy-washy *Peanuts* comic strip character, was always portrayed as a boy with an indomitable spirit. He regularly prepared, planned, and practiced—but somehow always found a new way to lose.

For one memorable moment, though, the round-headed kid seemed to pull it all together. Running a race, he found himself far ahead of the competition. Shocked by his own success and imminent victory, he began to fantasize about his coming glory. Throwing his head back and smiling from ear to ear, he ran faster than ever. Unfortunately, he was so preoccupied with his thoughts that he ran off the course, out of the stadium—and into his familiar slot of last place.

By now you've realized that following your family covenant isn't simply a sprint with a beginning and an end. It's a long-distance journey that requires care, work—and attention!

Keep your eyes on the prize: helping your children to fall in love with Jesus and to experience His abundant life. In the end, you'll realize you couldn't have spent that time more constructively.

Going Our Way?

As the story goes, an old Irishman was making his way through an ancient cemetery just outside of Dublin. Gazing at the headstones, he saw the following inscription:

Remember Me as You Go By,
For as You are So Once was I.
And as I am, So too Will You Be,
So Be Content to Follow Me.

The feisty gentleman couldn't resist. He took out a piece of paper and wrote the following words, which he later placed under a rock atop the granite marker:

To Follow You, I Am Content
I Only Wish I Knew Which Way You Went!

As believers in the Lord Jesus Christ, we can know where we're going. And as parents committed to writing and following intentional family covenants, we can know how we're getting there!

 POINT • OF • ACTION

Still have doubts about—or difficulties with—committing to a family covenant? Check out the "Troubleshooting" section at the end of this book. If that's not enough, let us know here at Focus on the Family (1-800-A-FAMILY) if we can be of further assistance. It would be our privilege to pray with you and help you tackle the task at hand.

CHAPTER 7

Helping Kids Reach the Next Level

Katie and Mark had been married for just over five years when their son, Nicholas, made his grand entrance into the world.

When Nicholas turned five, he began asking questions about faith. At first they were easy. Once he asked, "Where does God live?" Later he wanted to know about Christmas and Easter. He was always satisfied with a one- or two-sentence answer. But one night at dinner Nicholas stumped them.

"Why was I born?" he asked.

"We were really taken aback," Katie later said. "We knew he wasn't asking about the birds and the bees. He was asking something that went a lot deeper, and for which we really had no solid answer."

Katie and Mark stumbled along with a weak reply, but the exercise shook them. If Nicholas was asking these questions now, what would he be asking as a teenager?

Whether you're a "newbie" like Katie and Mark or an "old hand" at spiritual things, you may wonder exactly what your children need to learn about God—or even what they *can* learn. What should your family covenant ask of toddlers or teens? This chapter and the next can help you set age-appropriate goals you can target for the long term.

"It's Too Much!"

When you consider all that your children need to learn—the Bible, the nature of God and what He's done, how to have a personal relationship with Him, and what all of that means for their lives—it can seem as if you're standing behind a fully loaded dump truck as the driver raises the back. Out fall doctrine, parables, wisdom, history, truths, prophecy, miracles, guidelines for conduct, God's kingdom, faith, belief, sin and its consequences, laws, discipline, and character development. And that's only the beginning!

Don't panic. It's really not as overwhelming as it might seem. For one thing, you have your children for two to four years at each stage of development. It's going to take time. But if you plan your work and work your plan, you'll greatly increase your chances of success.

Some Basics

Let's look at some of the things you may already be doing: mealtime prayers of thanks, bedtime Bible stories and prayers, Advent calendars at Christmas, Sunday school, prayers for illnesses and "owies." All of these can teach your children that God is approachable, loves them, provides food, cares when they feel bad, and tells about Himself in the Bible.

If you're already doing some of these things, congratulations! It's a good start. To help you decide whether you need to go further, here are some facts about what most children can learn at various stages.

Ages 0-4: Laying the Foundation
Your key task in the earliest stage of your children's lives is to lay a solid foundation of love. They need to know that they're accepted,

wanted, and cherished. This is also the best time to build in them the knowledge of God's reality, care, and power.

When you protect and love children at this age by caring for their basic needs, they learn that they are loved and the world is a safe place. They need to know this is also true spiritually. So you need to demonstrate with actions and words that God is like you: He also cares for them, keeps them safe, and makes sure that their needs are met. When they hear and see this repeatedly, they begin to build a worldview with a Christian foundation that sets them up for life.

In these early years your kids are dependent on you to feed and nourish them spiritually. Pray simple, short prayers over them that affirm God's love and care. (Books like *Bedtime Blessings 1* and *Bedtime Blessings 2* by John Trent [Focus on the Family/Tyndale, 2009] provide plenty of creative ways to do this.)

As your children grow, they move toward the next stage, where they'll become more actively involved in their own faith and learning. On the way there, they'll enjoy the things you're doing together with them and God, such as praying, reading Bible storybooks, and singing songs. They'll begin to want to "do it myself" rather than having you do it all for them. They'll start to grasp some of the basics about God and the Christian faith: They'll understand certain things about how God wants them to be and behave, know that God loves them and made them (and everything else) on purpose, and know that they can talk to Him.

Here are some things about God that most children in the upper end of this age range are ready to learn:

- God exists.
- God loves you.
- Jesus loves you.
- God wants to take care of you.

- God created everything.
- God created you.
- God gave us the Bible.
- God's Son, Jesus, died for your sins so you can be with God; you can have a relationship with Him.

Ages 5-6: Establishing and Teaching About Relationships

Your key task during this stage is to help your children have a growing relationship with God and others. Thus far you've been doing everything for your children, but now they're ready for the next step where you take them to God and actively train them to do their part in the task of learning, doing, and growing. It's time to help them become committed to God and develop their own relationship with Him.

Age five to six is an important time of learning about relationships and how they work, with both God and people. Kids at this stage need to establish a strong understanding of why relationships are so important and how they affect all of us.

Children this age are no longer so passive. They're ready to be pulled into active involvement in their own development. It's important for them to learn that it's not just *your* relationship with God—it's *theirs* (just as they have their own relationships with other children). They can, for example, begin to say their own prayers, and they need to read regularly from their Bible storybooks with you.

At this stage, growing autonomy is the name of the game. If their life snapshots until now have always included you front and center, now they're starting to include their friends and growing social contacts—often with you in the background. Here are some tips on making those snapshots positive pictures.

- *Talk about how your kids like to be treated.* They need to learn *how* to have relationships with God and others.

- *Use your relationship and rapport with them.* Show them what a relationship with God is like. For example, help them see that if they never talked to you, or vice versa, you wouldn't know each other very well. It's the same with God.

- *Have them start saying their own prayers.* You can still help them decide what to pray for, but now they can pray for the things on their list in their own words. You could alternate—one night you pray, the next they do, gradually increasing the nights they do it.

- *Talk about reasons for obeying.* Children have already been working on obeying you; now they can understand that they obey because of their relationship with God—He wants them to. Always give them the reason for obedience: because God loves them and knows what's best.

- *Introduce the gospel.* Most children at this stage will be able to grasp the simple message of their relationship with God being broken because of sin; of Jesus, God's Son, dying in their place; of their need to accept what Jesus did; and of living with Him forever. They won't understand all of it, at least not in the same way they will as adults, but many children ask Jesus into their hearts at this age or younger. The Spirit of God draws them to Himself, and He knows when they're ready. (For more information on how to help your child begin a relationship with God, see *FaithLaunch* [Focus on the Family/Tyndale, 2008].)

Here are some things about God that most children at this age are ready to learn:

- God is your loving Father. He wants to guide, teach, love, protect, and provide for you.
- Jesus has always been with God and is God.

- God tells you about Himself, His Son, Jesus, and His plan for you in the Bible.
- God sent His Son, Jesus Christ, to die for you.
- God has prepared a place for you in heaven. Jesus is coming back for you.
- You can have a relationship with God by accepting what Jesus did for you.
- God wants to have a relationship with you.
- You can talk to God through prayer.

Ages 7-9: Giving Them Reasons for Their Faith

This is the "age of reason." Children are beginning to think for themselves. They want to know "why" and "how" and explore options. It's important to explain things to them in preparation for the next stage, when they'll start making their own decisions. If you don't know the answer, search for it with them. Teach them how to find answers and show them that you can always learn and grow.

Children also need *relational* reasons. That is, they need to experience the results of actively trusting their loving God. When they pray to find friends or for help on a test, show them the answers when they come. When they choose to tell the truth or not to steal, show them how it worked out because God's way works best. (For stories that make points like these, try audio albums of the *Adventures in Odyssey* radio series available from Focus on the Family.)

Here are some things to remember at this stage:

- *Explain your role.* Tell them that your job is to continue encouraging and loving them, but also to insist that they do their part. Their job is still to learn and take the next step. You'll be there to show them how and make sure they understand where they're going, and God is always nearby.

- *Encourage and try to answer your children.* They'll ask why certain behaviors are important, right, or wrong; why God seems to answer some prayers and not others; why some of their friends aren't Christians; and much more. You don't need to have a ready reply to every question; look for answers together.
- *Show them examples from the Bible that address their concerns.* Children at this age need to know that they can trust the Bible and God. Help them understand that many Bible stories can guide them in knowing how to live.
- *Prepare your children for what's coming.* Expect them to have very different concerns, speeds of learning, degrees of willingness to step out alone, and desire for your support. Whenever they move toward more autonomy, they're edging toward the next stage.

Here are some concepts most kids at this stage are ready to learn:

- You can be sure that God is real.
- God exists in three Persons: Father, Son, and Holy Spirit. This is called the "Trinity."
- God's character is true, honest, loving, compassionate, generous, selfless, forgiving, merciful, trustworthy, faithful, just, impartial, and holy.
- The Bible is true. It is God's Word, and you can trust it.
- God wants you to learn and study the Bible.
- You can trust God and turn your life over to Him.
- Church is God's idea. Jesus is the head of the church. At church you learn about God and encourage each other to follow Jesus.
- God wants you to share your faith.

Ages 10-12: Helping Them Make the Right Choices

This is a crucial time as kids learn what the Bible says about how they should live, what choices they need to make, and what God expects of them. They're moving toward greater independence in their spiritual lives. Your main goal is to ensure that, by the time they leave home, they've developed a maturing relationship with God.

These children are really beginning to think for themselves. Your job is to help them learn to make the right choices. You need to begin letting go and allow them to test their wings and make some decisions in the controlled, safe environment of home. Knowing your standards and how you arrived at them will give them the rationale for making good choices.

The snapshots that fill this section of your children's photo albums are beginning to show their growing experiences and confidence. You still appear in the background of some of the shots, but it's time to start moving out of the way. Here are some tips on doing that:

- *Encourage them to take more responsibility by easing them into it.* If you've been using bedtime as your time together with God, for instance, don't abandon it; change its function. Morph it gradually into a time to visit, to talk about what's happening at school, to discuss what your children want to pray about. When they can get through the prayer time without input from you, they're ready for you to pull back. They're getting personal with God.
- *Show your children how to find answers in the Bible.* Replace Bible storybooks with age-appropriate, full-text Bibles of their own. When they have questions, direct them to a part of the Bible that will help. Read the same passage yourself, then discuss what you've read. Let them know that the goal of Bible

reading is learning and application. But don't force it; trust God to work in their lives and speak to them.

- *Encourage participation in church activities by making it easy for them to get there.* Church is increasingly important to many children this age as they join clubs and make key friends. It can provide a safe place for them to explore autonomy in their faith.
- *Let your children see what's outside the Christian bubble.* They need exposure to other ideas in order to choose and defend their own. Help them discover what to do with new ideas and learn to compare them with Scripture. (For backup in this area, see these books by Lee Strobel with Rob Suggs: *The Case for Christ for Kids*, *The Case for Faith for Kids*, and *The Case for a Creator for Kids* [Zonderkidz, 2006].)
- *Share with your children what you're learning.* Your relationship with them is changing; you're becoming travelers on the same road. Ask them to pray about your concerns, such as work; ask them what concerns of theirs they want you to pray for.

Here are some concepts your children are ready to learn at this stage:

- Not everyone believes the truth about God, but there are ways you can respond to their objections.
- You can pray, read the Bible, and worship on your own or in a group.
- God's grace: You don't have to do it on your own. God is working in you by His Holy Spirit.
- You need to seek and follow God's will.
- God wants you to choose to commit your entire life and everything you have to Him.

- God wants you to choose His way because you love Him and want to be like Jesus.
- You need to learn how to resist Satan and temptation.
- You need to get involved in church and find your place in the body of Christ.

What's Next?

By the time your children leave this stage and head for their teens, they can know who they are and how they fit into God's story. With this foundation they can grow into people who want to know and learn more about the Christian life, grow in their relationship with God, and take responsibility for it.

As your children move toward their teens, they face greater temptations. The key is for them to know that their relationship with God is the cornerstone of the rest of their lives. With His help and yours, they can weather many storms and use the right tools to make good decisions.

 POINT • OF • ACTION

Reading together is a wonderful family activity no matter how old your kids are. Check your local Christian bookstore for ideas. Older children can read picture books to younger ones. As your kids move beyond simple stories, consider classics like The Chronicles of Narnia by C. S. Lewis and *Pilgrim's Progress* by John Bunyan.

While you're at the bookstore, compare children's Bibles and those for older kids. What are your children ready for? If possible, bring your kids back to the store and let them recommend storybooks and Bibles that appeal to them.

CHAPTER 8

Helping Teens Get Where They're Going

Adam, age 16, sits sullenly on the living room sofa. He rolls his eyes as Dad announces that the family is about to embark on "an exciting new way of doing things." Eight-year-old Maya's eyes widen while Dad describes a "family covenant for the next year" that seems to involve baking oatmeal-raisin cookies and turning them into object lessons. Adam looks anything but excited.

If it doesn't involve an iPod or a girlfriend or a steering wheel, Adam isn't interested these days. Watching the boy out of the corner of his eye, Dad pauses in his sales pitch and sighs. When it comes to faith training, has he already lost his son? How is this "spiritual journey" stuff supposed to work with anyone over the age of 12? Where does a kid with feet the size of rowboats need to walk faith-wise during the next year, and how can his parents nudge him in that direction?

Everything's Changed—Almost

Adam's dad isn't alone. Many parents wish the adolescent years were simply a continuation of the preteen process. They'd like to control everything their teen does. As you may have noticed, few teenagers share that view.

It's only normal: As an adolescent struggles to form an independent identity, he pulls away from the "Yes, Mommy" approach to decision making. And as the young person's need to take on greater responsibility increases in preparation for adulthood, it's vital that the "control center" begins to move from parent to offspring.

Whether we like it or not, the relationship is changing—and *must* change. We can't influence our teens in the way we did when they were younger. But we *can* choose to work *with* the process and not against it. That's why the most successful parents of teenagers will recognize the change, accept it, and write their family covenants accordingly, gradually transferring control and responsibility for choices and actions to their teens. These parents become coaches.

What's a Coach For?

Coaches guide, encourage, and teach. For a parent, the transition from governor to coach is made by slowly letting go during the teen years, giving more and more freedom as the child proves trustworthy. Instead of maintaining a viselike grip on the youngster's life until the last possible second when he leaves home, the wise parent shifts responsibility—each year putting a bit more onto the shoulders of the teen.

The timing of this shift is crucial. The parents of 13-year-old Derek, for example, know that he's ready to take on more responsibility for his own spiritual growth. He's so zealous, in fact, that kids at school call him "Bible boy." He even started an after-school prayer meeting in a classroom. Now is the time for Derek's folks to offer him a new challenge—a missions trip during spring break, perhaps.

By contrast, 15-year-old Brianna has always been more interested in surfing the Web than in searching the Scriptures. Her parents are helping her find Web sites that offer devotional readings, in the hope that she'll develop the habit of spending "quiet times" with God.

It wouldn't make sense for "Bible boy" Derek's parents to hover over his devotional life, planning his next 365 readings by chapter and verse and sitting on the edge of his bed to make sure he doesn't miss one. Nor would it be wise for webmistress Brianna's folks to simply hope that her lack of interest in Bible reading will somehow take care of itself. Demanding that Brianna muscle her way through Leviticus might foster only resentment and failure, but starting with her Internet enthusiasm just may work.

The parents of Derek and Brianna know these things because they understand that coaches need to be clear-eyed observers of their kids. They also understand that family covenants need to be written with a realistic view of the parent-teen relationship. Whether you're bursting with spiritual wisdom or feeling like you left it in your other suit, you won't get far in carrying out your family covenant unless you build a relationship with your teen.

Can You Relate?

Chris, a teenage caller to the *Life on the Edge LIVE!* radio show, explained why he wanted to honor his Christian upbringing:

> Well, "obey your father and your mother." It's the most
> important thing that I can think of. . . . If you're not obeying
> your mother and your father, then who are you going to run
> to? I mean, you can run to God and you can get comfort
> from Him, but God is just going to tell you to run back to

your parents and mend those open wounds. . . . [Our parents] have taken care of us. They love us. And I don't see why anybody would want to stray away from their parents. I love mine to death, and I would do anything for them.

Many parents wish they had that kind of relationship with their teens. It's not easy to achieve, often because of conflicts over everything from grades to tattoos to the need for taking showers. One way to minimize those battles is to choose them carefully.

Here are five questions to ask yourself when you need to decide whether to "stand your ground" or "keep the peace":

1. *Is my child's eternal destiny at stake here?* It's easy to forget, but the gospel boils down to a pretty simple statement: "Believe in the Lord Jesus, and you will be saved" (Acts 16:31).

2. *Am I upset because my teen is rejecting the Bible or because I feel rejected?* Is your child really discounting Scripture or just interpreting it in a way that differs from your own? Explain your position, but respect your teen's right to disagree—and try not to take it personally.

3. *Is this issue addressed in historic statements of what's essential in the Christian faith?* If not, it may be a matter of preference. For example, look at the Apostles' Creed to see what many believers have seen for centuries as non-negotiable. Hair length and music volume, it seems, are not mentioned.

4. *Is this worth risking our relationship?* Trying to force a teen to believe or behave can damage your ability to gain a hearing in the future. If the issue threatens a teen's safety, you might have to mark off boundaries and let the chips fall where they may. But if not, consider avoiding ultimatums in order to continue having a low-key, long-term influence.

5. *Do I need to leave this in God's hands?* When your teen seems headed in the wrong direction, anxiety and even panic are understandable. But sometimes it takes a hard knock to change a young person's mind, and administering those is best left to the One who does such things perfectly. Keep loving and praying for your teen. Like many adolescents, she may be tearing her faith apart in order to put it back together again in a form she can truly own.

Learning to Let Go

Much as we might like to cage or cocoon our kids to protect them from the world (or themselves), the day will come when they're on their own. The time-honored "As long as you live under my roof, you'll follow my rules" will be an empty threat. We know, deep down, that's the way it should be. But it's not an easy prospect to contemplate when an agnostic college professor, binge-drinking roommate, or cult-member coworker can get a teen off course in a hurry.

Chances are that you won't be there to "straighten things out" when your newly liberated teen faces challenges like these. How can you create a family covenant that helps to prepare your child for that not-too-distant future?

Here are three principles to keep in mind as you write and carry out your plan.

1. *Encourage your teen to own his faith.* You can't *make* your teen believe. But you can make it clear that faith is an individual decision, not something he or she can borrow or inherit from you. Include in your covenant's action steps an occasional conversation about what's really happening in your young person's life and heart. (To encourage your teen's growth, offer resources like the books *Stand: Core*

Truths You Must Know for an Unshakable Faith and *Stand Strong in College*, both by Alex McFarland [Focus on the Family/Tyndale, 2005 and 2007].)

2. *Give kids increasing freedom to make choices.* The second thing we can do to ready kids for independence is to let them make as many decisions as possible. It's great to help teens turn their beliefs into convictions, but we must go a step further and let them start *applying* those convictions, too.

"But it's risky to let kids make choices," you might say. And you'd be right. Our teens will never truly grow up unless we take those risks, however. The key is to minimize the risks.

Not every decision can be handed over to a young person, of course. You would never say "You decide" about whether to drop out of school, for example, or whether to drink. But in hundreds of other matters, where in fact you can live with either option, parents can avoid tumultuous battles and encourage growth by handing over the power of choosing.

3. *Give kids increasing responsibility.* The third way to prepare teens for independence is to hand them more responsibility. This means taking off the spiritual training wheels and letting kids pedal the straight and narrow for themselves, even if the ride is a bit wobbly.

Many of us tend to expect less of our children than they're capable of, especially when it comes to spiritual things. Rob, an eighth grader, is expected to practice the piano every day—but his parents wouldn't dream of asking him to commit to regular prayer or Bible reading. Candace, a high school junior, is a standout speech team member—but her folks assume that "giving her testimony" in church would be just too intimidating.

Joe White, in *Faith Training* (Tyndale, 1998), suggests that kids take on the following responsibilities at approximately the following ages:

Age 12—Regular youth group attendance

Age 13.5—Daily quiet times

Age 14—Small, peer-group Bible study

Age 15—Lifestyle witnessing to friends

Age 17—Intellectual preparation (e.g., apologetics) for college

Age 18—Summer missionary trip or serving/giving job

No two children are alike, of course; all mature at different rates. A lot of us might be surprised, however, at what teenagers can do.

What About Church?

As you update your family covenant, what goals should you set when it comes to church attendance for your teen?

Some adolescents can't stand to miss a single youth group meeting, Bible study, or retreat. Others would rather be skinned alive than darken a church door. You may want to set a minimum requirement for church attendance, but give your teen options beyond that point.

For instance, let him choose to attend Sunday school *or* a small discipleship group; allow her to pick youth choir *or* the church softball team. If your church's youth program isn't particularly strong and your teen wants to be part of the group a friend attends, let it happen. Kids who are forced to attend programs they loathe are prone to abandon church when they're on their own; kids who develop positive associations with church and a habit of regular, voluntary attendance are more likely to continue the practice.

If Your Teen Goes Off Course

If you're struggling with the pain of a prodigal, it may seem pointless to make any spiritual plans for your family. But take courage from your heavenly Father, who knows what it's like to deal with wayward children.

Realize that God understands your pain. One common characteristic in parents of prodigals is an overwhelming sense of failure. The parents feel these pangs deeply, even though many have done far more to encourage their children than was ever done for them by their own parents. Others live with the genuine guilt of knowing they could have done more when their children were younger. The more alone we feel in our pain, the more we need to lock our gaze onto the God who knows our hurt, sees our tears, and hears our sighs.

Seek support from others who have shared a similar pain. Nobody understands like someone who has been there. If you don't know any parents of prodigals, ask your pastor to connect you to one.

Get sound advice and wise counsel. Meet with your pastor, a youth pastor, or a counselor to devise a plan for helping your child— or at least staying connected with him or her.

Take appropriate, measured action to turn your teen back toward the light. For instance, if your teen has fallen in with the wrong crowd at school, maybe he needs to be moved to another school. If your teen refuses to participate in your church's youth program because it's "lame" and "boring," investigate alternatives that may be more appealing to him. If your relationship with him is strained, perhaps he would be willing to see a family counselor with you. If your teen is bothered by "hypocrites" in the church (a common teen complaint), make sure you're not one of them—that your actions match your words and you keep your promises.

Enlist the help of a mentor. An admired adult can help when adolescents turn away from the Lord. Rebellious teens might be willing to listen to a mentor even as they ignore Mom and Dad's guidance.

Emulate our heavenly Father's unconditional love. He said, "I have loved you with an everlasting love; I have drawn you with lovingkindness" (Jeremiah 31:3), and "Never will I leave you; never will I forsake you" (Hebrews 13:5). Communicate to your son or daughter often, "There's nothing you could do that would make me stop loving you."

Pray. Never give up.

At times, such as when your prodigal does something particularly hurtful, you may find yourself unable to summon much love. If that happens, don't berate yourself for being a bad parent; you're just an imperfect human being like the rest of us. But take your feelings honestly to the Lord in prayer, and ask once again for His love to fill you, along with His wisdom and patience.

A Faith That Lasts

In their book *Guiding Your Teen to a Faith That Lasts* (Discovery House, 1994), Kevin Huggins and Phil Landrum wrote, "Getting a teenager to make a commitment to Christianity is not the hard part. The hard part is helping him find in Christianity something that will motivate him to give his life to it."

As you help your teen become a true disciple of Jesus Christ, he will become motivated to give his life in service to God. There are, of course, no guarantees that your teen won't wander from the Lord. But writing and executing a family covenant that provides a solid foundation of belief and understanding of God's Word—and makes your relationship a top priority—is the best way to instill a faith that lasts a lifetime.

 ## POINT • OF • ACTION

Take a look in this chapter at Joe White's checklist of responsibilities most teens can handle at various ages. Based on your experience, would you change the list in any way? If so, how? Which of these benchmarks has your teen reached? Which would you like to reach in the next six months? What goals and action steps might help you get there?

Troubleshooting

Have questions about planning your journey? We're here to help.

What If I Have No Time?

If you're struggling to find time to spiritually train your children, you're not alone. Increased work hours and other pressures have played havoc with families. Even with a good balance of priorities, we still have a lot on our plates.

Don't despair, however. Spiritual training takes a lot less time than you think. In fact, it can be done in as little as one hour a week with the whole family and a few minutes of one-on-one time with each child five days a week. Did you know that if you spend just 20 minutes per week intentionally teaching your children from the time they're 4 until they're 15, they will have received over 190 hours of biblical training?

Some of this time can be taken from things you're already doing:

- Do you drive your kids to the gym or school? You can teach lessons of faith in the car.
- Do you put your kids to bed with a story? That time can become an opportunity to teach them about God's love.

- Do you eat meals—even one a week—with the family? You can use that time.
- Does your family like to have fun? "Family night" activities teach truths—for instance, blowing up balloons to help children understand why God is real even though He's invisible, like the air.

All of these and others can be easy-to-use times for carrying out your family covenant.

What If I Feel Inadequate—or Fail?

That's the best place to be. When you're weak, Christ can be your strength (Philippians 4:13). Only inadequate parents need apply—or need His adequacy.

To bolster your confidence, consider these things: First, you're not alone in making the decision to pass your faith down to your children. You may *feel* like the only one, but there are thousands with no more experience or any fewer doubts than you who are already doing it.

Second, remember the concept of "grace parenting." It's God's grace that makes us strong when we're weak (2 Corinthians 12:10), that gives us wisdom when we need it (James 1:5). God's grace is enough (2 Corinthians 12:9). It's available to help us accomplish anything He gives us to do, including spiritual training. We also need to trust Him to work in the hearts, minds, and lives of our children in the same way He's worked in us. Grace takes the pressure off and allows us to simply work at the task to the best of our ability, trusting God for strength, wisdom, and results. Tell Him your fears and doubts; then ask Him, by His grace, to teach you and give you wisdom and all you need to get the job done.

Third, remember that the big picture is formed from little ones. One snapshot at a time is all you need to focus on. As you provide positive snapshots day by day, you fill your children's lives with memorable moments.

What If I'm Doing It Alone?

You're not completely alone. God is working alongside you and the many others facing the same challenge.

Single and "spiritually single" parents face a daunting task with little support. But don't despair! "He who began a good work in you will carry it on to completion" (Philippians 1:6). God is working in you and your children.

The bigger your obstacles are, the more help from God you can count on. Here's the testimony of one single mom:

> I started out as a spiritually single mom and ended up a completely single mom. Throughout those years I thought there was little I could do to train my kids. After all, I had no emotional support from anyone. I certainly couldn't do after-dinner devotions. Nor could I take evenings for family activities with a spiritual emphasis. But there are more ways to impart faith lessons than just devotions, and more opportunities for activities than just the evening.
>
> Each night I prayed with the children as they lay in their beds. I had printed a verse on a 3"x 5" card and read the same verse every night for a week. After the verse, I sang hymns to them. These times were precious as we discussed all sorts of things there in the darkness of their rooms. . . .
>
> Our poverty provided faith lessons as we prayed for our

needs and watched God miraculously answer those needs some of the time, and at others how He simply sustained us as we struggled.

Yes, such lessons took two of us—me and God.

What If Our Children Are at Different Ages and Stages?

Many resources come with suggestions on how to make them work effectively for older and younger kids. Even with these helps, though, some families may have difficulty making some of the methods work. If this is your situation, your older children can take a supportive mentoring role in family activities. You can spend a little more time focusing on them during one-to-one interaction.

If you have teenagers, include them in the process of training the younger children. But also recognize that they have different needs. By the time your children reach the teen years, you're pretty much done forming their values. Now your role shifts to that of a coach. There are many resources available to help you in this role.

What If We're a Blended Family?

With a blended family (and any family) there are many unwritten rules. Yet if a mom and dad will plan as a team, these obstacles can become opportunities for growth. Blended families have more to draw on—different heritages and backgrounds. Bring all your "little pictures," and those of your children, to God and ask for His wisdom.

Dr. Robert Barnes, one of the United States' leading experts on blended families, recommends that blended families do exactly what you're doing with this book: Get a clear, prayed-over, talked-through, written-out parenting plan! You'll be glad you did, because there's nothing more unifying than having every family member fall in love with God.

What If My Own Spiritual Life Is Shaky?

You don't have to have unshakable faith to train your children. Even giants of the faith like Moses, Elisha, David, Peter, and Paul had times of questioning, doubt, or disappointment. A strong faith doesn't mean you never question or feel far from God.

In the middle of long-term doubts, serious questions about God, or times you just can't face things, the fact remains: God is, and He revealed Himself in the Bible saying He is love. Sometimes you just have to hold on to what the Bible says as if it were the only unshakable thing in the world. Feelings are not arbiters of truth; God is. Hang on to the basics: "For God so loved the world that he gave his one and only Son, that whoever believes in him shall not perish but have eternal life" (John 3:16).

If your doubts go even deeper and you're not sure you've ever received Jesus' gift of eternal life, it could be decision time. You *can* know for sure where you'll spend eternity. "If you confess with your mouth, 'Jesus is Lord,' and believe in your heart that God raised him from the dead, you will be saved. For it is with your heart that you believe and are justified, and it is with your mouth that you confess and are saved" (Romans 10:9-10). If you're ready to open that door, pray along these lines: "Dear God, I confess that You are Lord. Thank You so much for sending Jesus to die for me and pay the penalty for my sins. Please forgive me. Thank You for raising Him from the dead and defeating Satan. Thank You so much for saving me. Teach me to follow You. In Jesus' name, amen."

If you prayed that prayer for the first time, tell a loved one (or several) about it. And don't worry about being a new Christian when it comes to passing down your faith. Growing together with your children can be the most effective way to spiritually train them.

What If My Child Has a Learning Disability or Other Special Need?

If you are the parent of a severely handicapped child, you may tend to shy away from trying to give him or her an awareness of God and heaven. With little or no way of gauging your child's response, you may find yourself asking, "Am I really getting through?"

Although your child might not grasp the message of salvation, he or she *can* grasp the love of God. He or she can learn a great deal about God's love without needing to understand every aspect of doctrine.

Here's what one parent has to say:

When my daughter Emily was little, I had no idea how much she would ever know or grasp. She was born with Down's syndrome and was a masterpiece of God's hand. Daily I would talk to her about everything. "Emily, this is a can," I would say to her as I took a can of green beans from the grocery store shelf. "This is a pencil. It's made from wood. Wood comes from a tree that God made."

And I would look directly into her eyes and tell her, "Emily, you have Down's syndrome. That means God gave you something extra—an extra chromosome. And He made you exactly as He wanted you to be. You are special, made in His image."

When her brother was born three and a half years later, we named him Abraham and spent many hours praying for him. Emily heard all these prayers for her and for her brother. One day when Abraham was two, he crawled into bed with me. "Where's Emily?" I asked.

"In my bed," Abraham replied.

I sent Daddy to look, and sure enough, Emily was there. "What are you doing in Abraham's bed?"

"I sing and prayed."

"What?"

"Prayer, Jesus," she said.

And then we realized she was singing and praying for her brother.

Regardless of whether or not your child is able to understand, pray over him or her, read from the Bible, and sing hymns or other Christian songs to him or her. You can have confidence in God's love for your child as you try to give him or her an awareness of that love.

What If My Spouse and I Are from Different Church Backgrounds?

The key might be to change your focus from where you've come from to where you're going. What do you want for your children? Every tradition has positive things to offer. Take the best parts of both of your backgrounds and move forward with those elements.

For example, if one person's background includes a traditional, liturgical church with its rich use of ceremony to convey the teaching, then bring that forward and teach your children the wonderful depth and richness of that tradition. If the other spouse comes from a more casual, relaxed faith background, have him or her bring that more relational "everydayness" into the mix.

The key is to find what works for your children and to give them the solid foundation they will need to live for God and have a wonderful, fulfilling life.

What If I Don't See the Need for All the Facts and Doctrine? I Just Want My Children to Love God.

Knowledge deepens and informs love. The more your children know about God and the more they know how amazing and wonderful He is, the more reason they'll have to love Him. "Make every effort to add to your faith goodness; and to goodness, knowledge" (2 Peter 1:5).

If doctrine and biblical facts were all there was to it, Christianity would be boring indeed. But if emotion based on experience were all there was, your children would have trouble when "experience" said God wasn't worth loving. Your children need a solid foundation upon which to build their relationship with God, their understanding of His Word and principles, and their lives. Everything that God has shown us about Himself has practical application to our lives and relationship with Him.

What If We've Already Tried Something Like This and It Didn't Work?

It's a good thing Edison didn't quit trying to get his lightbulb to work! And more than 70 publishers rejected Dr. Seuss before his first book was accepted.

If you haven't failed, you haven't tried. The issue in following a family covenant isn't perfection; it's God-honoring persistence. It's starting again after struggles. Most attempts at training kids fail because parents don't have a plan, or they didn't have a plan that worked for their family.

If you have no goals and the going gets tough, or when you're trying to push something at your family instead of pulling together, it's easy to turn on the TV or "wait until a better day." Even with a covenant that matches your family, you'll have days when it just doesn't work.

Don't use a slip or even many slips as an excuse to quit. Reward whoever says, "Hey, we should do our family time!" with a "Great idea!" not a groan brought on by guilt. Thank God for the reminder of the importance of what you're doing, and get back in the battle.

Creating Your Family Covenant at a Glance

Step 1: Identify Your Values

What are your family's top four or five values? To answer that question, it may be helpful to think through some life-changing experiences your family has undergone. For example, the stress of a car accident or long illness might have helped you realize how important the value of peace is to you.

Once you've listed your most strongly held values, write them in the "Values" section of the worksheet at the end of this book.

Step 2: Write Your Mission Statement

With your family's help, draft a mission statement that's Christ-centered, action-oriented, and legacy-driven. Write it in the "Mission" portion of the worksheet at the end of this book. For examples of family and corporate mission statements, see Chapter 4.

Step 3: List Your Goals

Write three to five goals for spiritual development, aiming to fulfill them by this time next year. Make sure they're consistent with your overall mission and values. Write your goals in the "Goals" part of the worksheet.

Step 4: Write Your Action Steps

Create one or two action steps for each goal and add these to the "Action Steps" portion of the worksheet.

Step 5: Sign Your Covenant

Have all family members sign your spiritual agreement. Frame it if you like, and post it prominently in your home.

Celebrate the signing of this document. Set a date, perhaps six months or a year from now, when you'll celebrate your progress and adjust the covenant if needed. And share your covenant with a support group—Sunday school class, church small group, friends—so that those walking with you can help you fulfill your plan.

FOCUS ON THE FAMILY®

Welcome to the Family

Whether you purchased this book, borrowed it, or received it as a gift, we're glad you're reading it. It's just one of the many helpful, encouraging, and biblically based resources produced by Focus on the Family® for people in all stages of life.

Focus began in 1977 with the vision of one man, Dr. James Dobson, a licensed psychologist and author of numerous best-selling books on marriage, parenting, and family. Alarmed by the societal, political, and economic pressures that were threatening the existence of the American family, Dr. Dobson founded Focus on the Family with one employee and a once-a-week radio broadcast aired on 36 stations.

Now an international organization reaching millions of people daily, Focus on the Family is dedicated to preserving values and strengthening and encouraging families through the life-changing message of Jesus Christ.

Focus on the Family MAGAZINES

These faith-building, character-developing publications address the interests, issues, concerns, and challenges faced by every member of your family from preschool through the senior years.

For More INFORMATION

 ONLINE:
Log on to
FocusOnTheFamily.com
In Canada, log on to
FocusOnTheFamily.ca

 PHONE:
Call toll-free:
800-A-FAMILY
(232-6459)
In Canada, call toll-free:
800-661-9800

| FOCUS ON THE FAMILY MAGAZINE | FOCUS ON THE FAMILY CLUBHOUSE JR.™ Ages 4 to 8 | FOCUS ON THE FAMILY CLUBHOUSE® Ages 8 to 12 | FOCUS ON THE FAMILY CITIZEN® U.S. news issues |

Rev. 12/08

More Great Resources
from Focus on the Family®

FaithLaunch: A Simple Plan to Ignite Your Child's Love for Jesus
John Trent, Ph.D. and Jane Vogel
As a Christian parent, your number-one priority is to see your children put their faith in Christ. *FaithLaunch* shows you step-by-step how to prepare them to make an informed decision to follow Jesus, or confirm a decision they already made. This book includes three *Adventures in Odyssey*® audio stories to reinforce the lessons. Paperback plus CD.

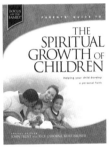

Parents' Guide to the Spiritual Growth of Children
General Editors: John Trent, Ph.D., Rick Osborne, Kurt Bruner
Passing on a heritage of faith to children is an incredible privilege God gives to parents. And now there's a comprehensive tool to help make it easy! Dozens of simple, practical ways are provided to develop Christian values and make faith in God part of your child's life. Paperback.

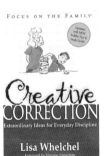

Creative Correction
Lisa Whelchel
Lisa Whelchel offers creative solutions for parents who are out of ideas and desperate for new, proven approaches to discipline. In addition to advice on topics such as sibling conflict and lying, Whelchel offers a biblical perspective and down-to-earth encouragement to parents who are feeling overwhelmed. Paperback.

FOR MORE INFORMATION

Online:
Log on to FocusOnTheFamily.com
In Canada, log on to focusonthefamily.ca.

Phone:
Call toll free: 800-A-FAMILY
In Canada, call toll free: 800-661-9800.

BPZZXP1